Designs of Chinese Buildings, Furniture, Dresses, Machines and Utensils.

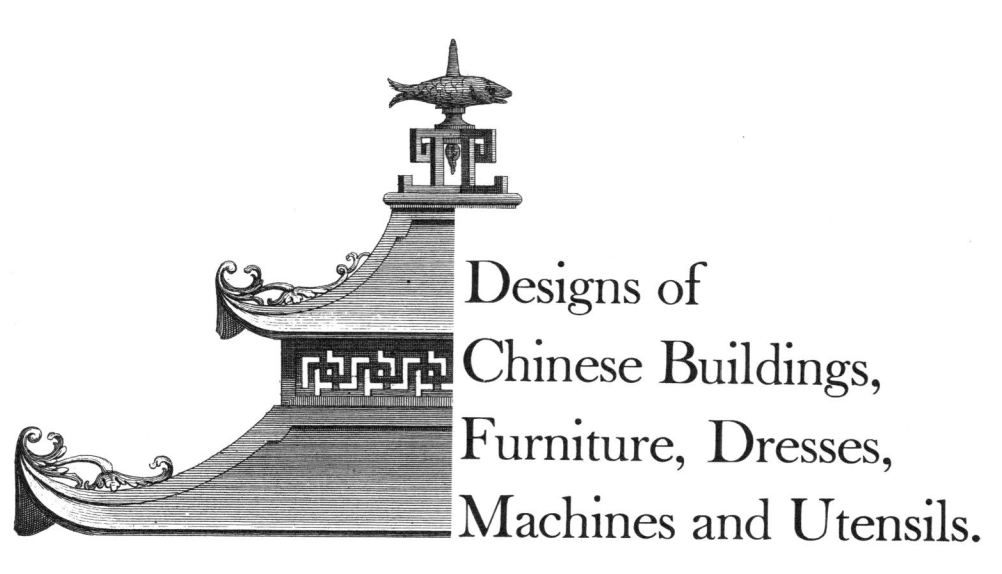

BY WILLIAM CHAMBERS
First published London 1757

ARNO PRESS
A New York Times Company
New York • 1980

Reprint edition 1980 by Arno Press, Inc.
LC 80-932
ISBN 0-405-08348-3
Manufactured in the United States of America

DESIGNS

OF

CHINESE

BUILDINGS, FURNITURE, DRESSES, MACHINES, and UTENSILS.

Engraved by the Best Hands,

From the ORIGINALS drawn in CHINA

BY

Mr. CHAMBERS, Architect,

Member of the Imperial Academy of Arts at FLORENCE.

To which is annexed,

A DESCRIPTION of their TEMPLES, HOUSES, GARDENS, &c.

LONDON:

Published for the AUTHOR, and sold by him next Door to Tom's Coffee-house, Russel-street, Covent-Garden: Also by Mess. Dodsley, in Pall-mall; Mess. Wilson and Durham; Mr. A. Millar, in the Strand, and Mr. R. Willock, in Cornhill.

MDCCLVII.

TO HIS

ROYAL HIGHNESS

GEORGE

PRINCE OF WALES,

THE FOLLOWING

DESIGNS

ARE MOST HUMBLY DEDICATED

By his Royal Highneſs's

Moſt dutiful, and

Moſt obedient Servant,

WILLIAM CHAMBERS.

LIST

OF THE

SUBSCRIBERS.

His Royal Highneſs the Prince of Wales.
Her Royal Highneſs the Princeſs Dowager of Wales.
His Royal Highneſs the Duke.

A.

Sir John Armitage, Bar.
Thomas Adderley, Eſq;
Mr. Alken, Carver.
Mr. John Adams, Architect.
Mr. James Adams.

B.

His Grace the Duke of Bedford.
Her Grace the Dutcheſs of Bedford.
His Grace the Duke of Bridgewater.
Right Honourable the Earl of Bute.
Right Honourable the Earl of Bleſſington.
Right Honourable the Counteſs of Bleſſington.
Right Honourable Lord Bruce.   4 Sets.
Right Honourable Lord Blakeney.
Right Honourable Lord Barnard.
Right Rev. Lord Biſhop of Bangor.
Sir Charles Bingham, Bar.
Honourable Richard Bateman.
Honourable William Bouvery.
Honourable Mr. Bruce.
Honourable Rr. Brudenell.
Thomas Brand, Eſq;   4 Sets.
William Baggot, Eſq;
Lyde Brown, Eſq;   2 Sets.
Rev. Mr. Boſworth.
Samuel Blakwell, Eſq;
John Blair of Dronſkay, Eſq;
Thomas Brand, Eſq;

C.

Right Honourable the Earl of Cardigan.   2 Sets.
Right Honourable the Counteſs of Cardigan.   2 Sets.
Right Honourable Earl of Cheſterfield.
Right Honourable Counteſs of Cheſterfield.
Right Honourable Lord Viſcount Charlemont.   4 Sets.
Right Honourable Lord Fred. Cavendiſh.
Right Honourable Lord Carpenter.
Honourable General Conway.
Honourable Francis Caulfield.
——— Cooper, Eſq;
Captain Craig.
John Gilbert Cooper, Eſq;
Mr. Thomas Churchil.
Archibald Crawfurd of Ardmilton, Eſq;
Signor J. Bap. Chipriani.
John Chambers, Eſq;
Mr. Thomas Clark.
Charles Cox, Eſq;

D.

Right Honourable Lord Viſcount Downe.
Right Honourable Lord Viſcount Dungarvan.
Honourable Mr. Duff.
James Dawkins, Jun. Eſq;
Peter Delme, Eſq;
Meſſrs. Du Val.   2 Sets.
Mr. Dalton.

E.

Right Honourable Lord Edgcumb.   2 Sets.

F.

Right Honourable Lord Foley.
Sir Mathew Fetherſton Haugh, Bar.
Henry Fox, Eſq;
Rev. Mr. Fowler.
Brice Fiſſier, Eſq;

G.

Right Honourable Earl of Gower.
Sir Harry Gray, Bar.
Honourable James Grenville.
Colonel Gray.
Thomas Gilbert, Eſq;
James Garland, Eſq;
Nathaniel Garland, Eſq;

H.

His Grace the Duke of Hamilton.
Right Honourable the Earl of Huntingdon.
Right Honourable the Earl of Holderneſs.
Right Honourable Lady Ann Hamilton.
Sir Charles Hotham, Bar.   4 Sets.
Thomas Hollis, Eſq;
William Gerard Hamilton, Eſq;
John Hall Stevenſon, Eſq;
John Harding, Jun. Eſq;
William Hall, Eſq;
Mr. Hone, Painter.
Leſcoe Hide, Eſq;   2 Sets.

I.

Right Honourable the Earl of Ilcheſter.
——— Jones, Eſq;
Charles Jennens, Eſq;
Samuel Ibbeſon, Eſq;
James Ingliſh, Eſq;

K.

Sir Thomas Kennedy of Kullein, Bar.
David Kennedy of Kirkmichael, Esq;
Ralph Knight, Esq;
William Kent, Esq;
Mr. Kirby, Master of Perspective to His Royal Highness the Prince of Wales.
David Killican, Esq;

L.

Right Honourable Lord George Lenox.
Honourable Sir Richard Littleton, Knight of the Bath.
Sir Robert Long, Bar.
Sir James Lowther, Bar.
Dr. Robert Lynch, M. D.
Peter Lascelles, Esq;
Mr. Leake, Bookseller at Bath.
Mr. Leake, Jun.
William Lock, Esq;
Michael Leigh, Esq;
Mr. James Livingston.

M.

Sir William Maxwell of Munreith, Bar.
Hervy Mildmay, Esq;
George Maddison, Esq;
Edward Murphey, Esq;
Rev. Mr. Marlay.
Mr. George Mercer.   2 Sets.
Mr. G. Moser.
Richard Mitchel, Esq;
Miss Barbara Marsden.
———— Mitchel, Esq;
Mr. James Morris.
———— Monk, Esq;
Thomas Miller, Esq;

N.

Right Honourable the Earl of Northumberland.
Colonel Noel.
William Northie, Esq;
Robert Nugent, Esq;

O.

Right Rev. Lord Bishop of Ossory.
———— Offley, Esq;

P.

His Grace the Duke of Portland.
Her Grace the Dutchess of Portland.
Right Honourable the Earl of Pembroke.
Right Honourable Lord Viscount Powerscourt.
Roger Palmer, Esq;
Mr. James Payne, Architect.
George Pitt, Esq;
Edward Popham, Esq;
Joseph Pratt, Esq;

R.

His Grace the Duke of Richmond, &c.
Most Honourable the Marquis of Rockingham.
Mr. J. Reinolds, Painter.
Thomas Ryves, Esq;
Mr. Joseph Rose.
John Rich, Esq;
Mr. Ride, Builder.

S.

Honourable Sir Wm. Stanhope, Knight of the Bath.
Sir John Swinburn, Bar.
Sir Thomas Stapleton, Bar.
———— Stopford, Esq;
Mr. Smith, Professor of Moral Philosophy in the University of Glasgow.
Philip Stanhope, Esq;
John Silvester Smith, Esq;
Mr. Thomas Sandby, Draughtsman to His Royal Highness the Duke.
Mr. Paul Sandby, Painter.
Mr. Spencer, Painter.
Thomas Stevens, Esq;
Thomas Scrope, Esq;
John Sawbridge, Esq;
David Sandberg, Esq;

T.

Right Honourable Earl Temple.
Right Honourable the Earl of Tylney.
Honourable Charles Townshend.
Charles Turner, Esq;
Walter Taylor, Esq;
William Tash, Esq;
Mr. P. Tollot.

W.

Honourable John Ward.
Honourable Horace Walpole.
Robert Wood, Esq;   2 Sets.
Mr. John Vardie, Architect.
Mr. J. Wilton.
Mr. Joseph Wilton, Sculptor.

Y.

William Yong, Esq;

PREFACE.

IT is difficult to avoid praising too little or too much. The boundless panegyricks which have been lavished upon the Chinese learning, policy, and arts, shew with what power novelty attracts regard, and how naturally esteem swells into admiration.

I AM far from desiring to be numbered among the exaggerators of Chinese excellence. I consider them as great, or wise, only in comparison with the nations that surround them; and have no intention to place them in competition either with the antients, or with the moderns of this part of the world: yet they must be allowed to claim our notice as a distinct and very singular race of men; as the inhabitants of a region divided by it's situation from all civilized countries; who have formed their own manners, and invented their own arts, without the assistance of example.

EVERY circumstance relating to so extraordinary a people must deserve attention; and though we have pretty accurate accounts of most other particulars concerning them, yet our notions of their architecture are very imperfect: many of the descriptions hitherto given of their buildings are unintelligible; the best convey but faint ideas; and no designs worth notice have yet been published.

THESE which I now offer to the publick are done from sketches and measures taken by me at Canton some years ago, chiefly to satisfy my own curiosity. It was not my design to publish them; nor would they now appear, were it not in compliance with the desire of several lovers of the arts, who thought them worthy the perusal of the publick, and that they might be of use in putting a stop to the extravagancies that daily appear under the name of Chinese, though most of them are mere inventions, the rest copies from the lame representations found on porcelain and paper-hangings.

WHATEVER is really Chinese has at least the merit of being original: these people seldom or never copy or imitate the inventions of other nations. All our most authentick relations agree in this point, and observe that their form of government, their language, characters, dress, and almost every other particular belonging to them, have continued without change for thousands of years: but their architecture has this farther advantage that there is a remarkable affinity between it and that of the antients, which is the more surprising as there is not the least probability that the one was borrowed from the other.

PREFACE.

IN both the antique and Chinese architecture the general form of almost every composition has a tendency to the pyramidal figure: In both, columns are employed for support; and in both, these columns have diminution and bases, some of which bear a near resemblance to each other; fretwork, so common in the buildings of the antients, is likewise very frequent in those of the Chinese; the disposition observed in the Chinese Ting † is not much different from that in the Peripteros of the Greeks; the Atrium, and the Monopteros and Prostyle temples, are forms of building that nearly resemble some used in China; as the Chinese manner of walling is upon the same principle with the Revinctum and Emplecton described by Vitruvius. There is likewise a great affinity between the antient utensils and those of the Chinese; both being composed of similar parts combined in the same manner.

Though I am publishing a work of Chinese Architecture, let it not be suspected that my intention is to promote a taste so much inferiour to the antique, and so very unfit for our climate: but a particular so interesting as the architecture of one of the most extraordinary nations in the universe cannot be a matter of indifference to a true lover of the arts, and an architect should by no means be ignorant of so singular a stile of building: at least the knowledge is curious, and on particular occasions may likewise be useful; as he may sometimes be obliged to make Chinese compositions, and at others it may be judicious in him to do so. For though, generally speaking, Chinese architecture does not suit European purposes; yet in extensive parks and gardens, where a great variety of scenes are required, or in immense palaces, containing a numerous series of apartments, I do not see the impropriety of finishing some of the inferiour ones in the Chinese taste. Variety is always delightful; and novelty, attended with nothing inconsistent or disagreeable, sometimes takes place of beauty. History informs us that Adrian, who was himself an architect, at a time when the Grecian architecture was in the highest esteem among the Romans, erected in his Villa, at Tivoli, certain buildings after the manner of the Egyptians and of other nations.

THE buildings of the Chinese are neither remarkable for magnitude or richness of materials: yet there is a singularity in their manner, a justness in their proportion, a simplicity, and sometimes even beauty, in their form, which recommend them to our notice. I look upon them as toys in architecture: and as toys are sometimes, on account of their oddity, prettyness, or neatness of workmanship, admitted into the cabinets of the curious, so may Chinese buildings be sometimes allowed a place among compositions of a nobler kind.

IT may be objected that the suburbs of a sea-port cannot furnish the proper means for deciding the taste of a nation. But when we reflect that Canton is one of the most considerable cities in Asia, and in many respects inferiour to none in China, that objection will lose much of it's weight. Had I been ad-

---

† A Ting is the great hall of a house, the room in which guests are entertained, the hall where the Mandarins sit in judgment; also the great halls in a Pagoda or temple. See plate 2. and 3. &c.

mitted

PREFACE.

mitted to range over the whole empire, no doubt I could have swelled my work with more examples: but if I may be allowed to judge from such imperfect things as Chinese paintings, they would all have been in the same stile; and, with regard to their general form and disposition, nearly resembling those contained in this work. Besides, my intention being only to give an idea of Chinese architecture, not designs of particular buildings, any farther than they contribute to that purpose, it were a trespass on the patience of the publick to offer many examples, when a few properly chosen are sufficient. I have even omitted the greatest part of those I met with in Canton, either because they were mere repetitions of the same thing, or presented nothing remarkable.

Du Halde observes that there is such a resemblance between the cities of China, that one is almost sufficient to give an idea of all; and the same remark may be made on their buildings: for in all the paintings I ever saw, which were very numerous, and in all the descriptions I ever read, I do not remember to have met with any forms of building greatly differing from those which I have represented.

To my designs of Chinese buildings I have added some of their furniture, utensils, machines, and dresses. Those of the furniture were taken from such models as appeared to me the most beautiful and reasonable: some of them are pretty, and may be useful to our Cabinet-makers.

The Chinese utensils, notwithstanding the humble purposes to which they are applied, deserve to be considered. I have therefore inserted two plates of them in this work: several of the thoughts are ingenious, the forms simple and elegant, and the ornaments natural, and judiciously applied. They are, as I before observed, composed in the spirit of the antique; but want that graceful turn observable in the works of some of the ancient and modern Europeans; which is owing to the Chinese being less expert in the practical part of design than the Europeans.

An accident hath prevented my giving more designs of Chinese machines; but our knowledge of mechanics in Europe so far exceeds theirs that the loss is not of much consequence. Among them I have inserted several of their boats.

It was not my intention to touch on any thing that did not immediately belong to my profession. However, as I had by me designs of the Chinese dresses, drawn with a good deal of accuracy, I judged it would not be amiss to publish them, as I believe they are the exactest that have hitherto appeared. Some of them are picturesque, and may be useful in masquerades, and other entertainments of that kind, as well as in grotesque paintings.

The Chinese excell in the art of laying out gardens. Their taste in that is good, and what we have for some time past been aiming at in England

PREFACE.

England, though not always with success. I have endeavoured to be distinct in my account of it, and hope it may be of some service to our Gardeners.

The Plates are engraved by some of the most eminent English masters, who in their different branches are inferiour to none in Europe; and I have spared no expence to make the performance complete.

I cannot conclude without observing that several of my good friends have endeavoured to dissuade me from publishing this work, through a persuasion that it would hurt my reputation as an Architect; and I pay so much deference to their opinion, that I should certainly have desisted, had it not been too far advanced before I knew their sentiments: yet I cannot conceive why it should be criminal in a traveller to give an account of what he has seen worthy of notice in China, any more than in Italy, France, or any other country; nor do I think it possible that any man should be so void of reason as to infer that an Architect is ignorant in his profession, merely from his having published designs of Chinese buildings.

OF THE
TEMPLES
OF THE
CHINESE.

THERE are at Canton a great number of temples, by the Europeans commonly called Pagodas. Many of these are very small, consisting only of one room; others have a court surrounded with porticos, at the upper end of which is a *Ting*, where the idols are placed; and some few are composed of several courts, encompassed with porticos and cells for Bonzes, and having different halls for the reception of idols. These, properly speaking, are convents; and some of them have a great number of Bonzes belonging to them, who are bound by particular vows, and live under strict regulations.

THE most considerable among these is the Pagoda of Ho-nang in the southern suburb, of which Plate I. † is a plan. It occupies a large extent of ground, and contains, besides the idol-temples, lodging-rooms and other conveniences for two hundred Bonzes, with hospitals for a great many animals, a large kitchen-garden, and a burying ground, where priests and animals are promiscuously interred, both being equally honoured with monuments and inscriptions.

THE first thing that presents itself is a very large court with a triple avenue of trees, that leads to an open vestibule A, to which you ascend by a flight of steps B. From this vestibule you enter into a second C, where are four Colossal-figures of stucco, seated, and holding in their hands various emblems. This vestibule opens into another large court D, which is surrounded with colonnades E, and cells for the Bonzes F: in it are placed four pavillions G, standing on basements, and consisting each of two stories. These are the temples; both stories are full of idols, and in them the Bonzes perform their religious ceremonies. At the four angles of the court are four

Description of the Pagoda of Ho-nang, Plate I.

---

† I do not pretend to give this as a very accurate plan of that building: exact measures of Chinese structures are of small consequence to European Artists; and it is a matter of great difficulty to measure any publick work in China with accuracy, because the populace are very troublesome to strangers, throwing stones, and offer other insults.

other

2 *Of the* Buildings *of the* Chinese.

other pavillions H, in which are the apartments of the superiour Bonzes; and under the colonnades among the cells are four halls I, where idols are placed.

To the right and left of this large court are two small ones K, surrounded with buildings: the one contains the kitchens L, and the refectories M; the other the hospitals beforementioned N.

With regard to the elevation of the great court, I have omitted giving a design thereof; because to be of a proper size it would occupy at least three Plates. However Plate II. will give a sufficient idea of it. The pavillions are of various forms: but none of them very different from the one in that Plate; and the colonnades also bear nearly the same proportion to the pavillions as there. The cells of the Bonzes are of brick-work, very small, and without any other light than what comes in at the door. The bodies of the pavillions are of the same materials; and the columns that surround them, as well as those of the colonnades, are of wood, with marble bases. The buildings are all covered with tiles, made of a coarse sort of porcelain painted, green and glazed.

The same disposition is observed in all temples of this kind; and, if considered abstractedly from the three pavillions that occupy the middle of the great court, may serve to give an idea of the distribution in all Chinese buildings of large extent. The imperial palace, those of the princes of the blood, the palaces of the Mandarins, and the *Kong-Quaen*, or inns for the reception of the Literati, are all distributed nearly in this manner, as will appear by the annexed citations taken from Du Halde*; the principal difference being in the number and size of the courts.

The

---

* P. 17. Vol. 2. Although the description of the palace in the beginning of this work may seem sufficient, yet I shall here add several other particulars, in the words of one of the Missionaries, who had the honour to be admitted into the Emperour's presence, and to salute him in his own apartment. It consists, says he, of an astonishing collection of buildings, and a long series of courts, porticos, and gardens, which altogether form a whole truly magnificent.

As the southern gate is never opened but for the Emperour, we came in by that facing the East, which leads into a vast court on the South-side of the palace. This court is a quadrangle, whose length is double it's breadth; being two hundred geometrical paces from North to South. It is paved with large bricks, and the walks are laid with broad flat stones. *At each end is a large oblong building, with a double roof*, the ground-story of which has three entrances, like the gates of cities. Before we entered the next court, we came to a canal almost dry, running parallel to the walls of it from East to West. Over this canal we passed by one of the six marble bridges built towards the middle, facing five gates arched and open, which support a *large building with a double roof*; the diameter whereof is upwards of twenty geometrical paces. At each end of the bridge leading to the middle-gate, are two large columns of white marble, placed on a broad pedestal, and surrounded with a balustrade of the same material; the columns having on their base two lions, each seven or eight foot high, which seem both to have been cut out of the same block.

Passing northward through the gates into this second court, which is in length about a hundred geometrical paces, and fifty in breadth, you find at the entrance two other white marble columns, adorned with dragons in Relievo, having each two small wings, below a capital which is flat and very broad. Out of this you pass into a third court, twice the length of the second, and a little broader: the entrance is through five gates, like those already described, with a building over them of the same form. These gates are very thick, and covered with plates of iron, fastened with rows of brass nails, whose heads are bigger than a man's fist. *All the buildings of the palace are placed on a Basement of the height of a man, built of a reddish grey marble, ill polished, and adorned with mouldings. All these courts are surrounded with very low buildings, covered with yellowish tiles. At the bottom of this court there is a pretty long building,* flanked with two pavillions, which are joined to *two wings terminated by two other pavillions like the first, being double roofed, and surrounded with galleries, as are likewise the wings and the building at the bottom of the court,* which is raised on a plat-form of brick (with it's parapet and little embrasures) about thirty five foot high; the base of the plat-form rises six foot above the pavement, and is of marble. In this plat-form are three arched gates like the former; with this difference that the nails and iron-work are gilt, &c.

After

Of the Buildings of the Chinese.

THE Chinese have not, as the antients had, certain forms of building appropriated to sacred purposes. The particular kind of structure which they call *Ting*, or *Kong*, is used indifferently in all sorts of edifices. We meet with it in almost every temple, in all their palaces, over the gates of cities, and in all buildings where magnificence is aimed at.

I have seen four sorts of these *Tings* in different parts of Canton; three of them in temples, and the fourth in several gardens.

<small>Different forms of *Tings*.</small>

THE most common form used in temples is that represented Plate II, which is almost an exact copy from one in the Cochin-China Pagoda, in the eastern suburb. I have measured several of this sort, and found so much difference in their proportions, that I believe they do not work by any certain rule; but that every artist varies his measures at pleasure.

IN the design which I have given, the building is raised on a basement (as all of them are) and the ascent to it is by three flights of steps. It is of a square figure, and surrounded with a colonnade composed of twenty columns, that support a roof, terminated by a wooden rail which incloses a gallery, or passage, running all round the second story.

THE second story is likewise square, and of the same dimensions with the first. It is finished with a roof of a construction peculiar to the Chinese; the angles of which are enriched with ornaments of sculpture representing dragons.

After we had passed through these three courts, which are remarkable for nothing but their extent, we entered into a fourth, which is about fourscore geometrical paces square and exceedingly agreeable. *It is surrounded with porticos, interrupted from space to space by little open halls,* somewhat higher than the porticos, to which the ascent is by steps of white marble. Through this court runs a little canal, lined with white marble, the sides of which are adorned with balustrades of the same material; and over it are four or five bridges, each of one arch, built of white marble, and enriched with mouldings and basso relievos. *At the bottom of the court is a large and magnificent hall, to which you mount by three flights of steps, adorned with balustrades.*

The fifth court is nearly of the same form and size; but is nevertheless somewhat more striking. It contains a large Perron, or flight of steps, having three landing places enclosed with balustrades: this Perron occupies near half the length of the court, and two thirds of it's breadth: it is about eighteen foot high, built on a base of Siam marble about six foot high; to the top of which you mount by three flights of steps, that in the middle being larger than the other two. At the foot of the Perron, near the principal flight of steps just mentioned, stand two large lions of bronze; and at the top of it are placed eight large vases of the same metal, each being about seven foot high. This Perron is before a *large and magnificent hall*, &c.

Afterwards we pass'd through two other courts, very little different from the last described one: at the end of the second we were conducted through a door on the right hand into another court about two hundred paces long, being a kind of Hippodrome; at *the end of which on the left hand we entered a great open hall,* where we found guards, and waited for some time for the Mandarin appointed to conduct us into the apartment of the Emperour. Him we followed through a ninth court, something less than the former, but at least as sumptuous. *At the end of it appears a large building* of an oblong figure, *having a double roof* covered with yellow varnished tiles like the preceding. This is the palace where the Emperour's apartment is, to which there leads a causey, raised about five or six foot high, inclosed with balustres of white marble, and paved with the same, &c.

Vol. 1. p. 118. The palaces of the Emperour's children, and the other princes of the blood, are very neat within, very large, and built at a considerable expence: the same design is observed in them all, both as to the body of the work and the embellishments. *They consist of a series of courts, adorned on the sides with buildings, and in front with a varnished hall raised on a plat-form three or four foot high*, which is faced with great blocks of hewn stone, and paved with large bricks, &c.

Vol. 2. p. 63. The *Kong-Quaen* are sometimes large and sometimes small, and some of them are handsome and commodious enough. From that of Canton, which is one of the common sort, one may judge of the rest: it is of a moderate size, *consisting of two courts, and two principal buildings, one of which, at the bottom of the first court, is a Ting, or large open hall for receiving visits; the other, standing at the end of the second court, is divided into three parts; that in the middle serving for a saloon, or antichamber to the two great rooms that are on the sides, with each a closet behind. This disposition is observed in most of the houses belonging to persons of distinction in China,* &c.

The

THE breadth of the building, meafuring from the exterior furface of the columns, is equal to the whole height; and the diameter of the body, or cell, is two thirds of the whole breadth: the height of the order is equal to two thirds of the diameter of the cell; and the height of the fecond ftory is two thirds of the height of the firft. The columns are nine diameters high; their bafes two; and the beams and confoles that occupy the place of the capitals are one, which is likewife the height of the fret-work that runs round the whole colonnade, under the firft roof, and forms a fort of frife.

THE fecond kind of *Ting* differs fo little from that juft defcribed, that I thought it needlefs to give a defign of it. The lower ftory is exactly the fame; and there is no other difference in the fecond, but that it has neither gallery nor baluftrade round it; the roof that covers the colonnade being carried clofe to the walls.

THE third fort is reprefented in Plate III. fig. 2. The defign is taken from various buildings of that kind which I faw at Canton; but chiefly from one of the pavillions in the pagoda of Ho-nang. The firft ftory differs very little from that in the firft defcribed Ting; but the fecond has on two fronts columns that project and form covered galleries. I have feen fome of thefe buildings where the colonnade was continued quite round the fecond ftory; but the form of thefe is not fo agreeable as that which I have reprefented.

THE general proportions of this defign are very little different from thofe of Plate II. The columns in the firft ftory are about eight diameters high; their bafes are one diameter; and at the top of each fhaft, except on the angular columns, are eight confoles, forming a very clumfy kind of capital, which is a kind of ornament very frequent in Chinefe buildings, though by no means pleafing to the eye. The diameter of the fecond order of columns is about four fifths of that of the firft; and the columns are fix and a half diameters high, without bafes. Under the fecond roof runs an open fret, compofed of circles and fquares alternately difpofed: the angles of both roofs are enriched with ornaments, reprefenting monfters and foliages; and on the top of the fecond roof are two dolphins, one at each end, and in the middle a large fleuron refembling a tulip.

THESE three forms are more frequently met with than any other in their temples; particularly in thofe of large dimenfions: in the fmaller ones the defign reprefented in Plate III. fig. 1. is common; fometimes, as in that defign, fhutting in front with folding doors, and having four projecting columns that form a portico, fomewhat in the manner of a proftyle temple; and at other times entirely open in front, having only four columns to fupport the roof.

Other forms of Temples.

I found at Canton fome other figures of temples; but none that appeared to me worth copying, except two very fmall wooden buildings, that ftood in the courts of a pagoda in the weftern fuburb; of which fig. 1. and 2. Plate IV. are defigns. Thefe ferved to cover two large iron veffels, in which the Chinefe

facrifice

sacrifice gilt paper to their idols on their festivals. Both were of an octagonal figure, and each composed of eight columns, supporting a roof terminated with a lantern and other ornaments, as expressed in the design. Fig. 1. is somewhat raised, and surrounded with steps; it's columns are adorned with bases of a profile not very different from the Attic; and under the roof, between the intercolumnations, runs a frise on which are inscriptions in large Chinese characters. The lantern is an octagon, covered with a roof shaped like an inverted cymatium, and finished with an ornament composed of a little globe surrounded with leaves and flowers. Fig. 6. Plate V. is the plan of this building.

Fig. 2. is raised on a basement, and surrounded with an entrelas of brickwork *. It's columns have no bases, and under the first roof runs an open fret composed of lozenges interwoven. The lantern consists of eight little columns, without base or capital, that support a roof formed like a cone, and adorned with eight dolphins, one over each column. The building is finished with a perforated ball, on the top of which is a flower. Fig. 4. Plate V. is the plan of it. The proportions of these temples may be gathered from the designs to which I have prefixed a scale of modules.

OF THE

TOWERS.

THE towers called by the Chinese *Taa*, and which the Europeans call likewise pagodas, are very common in China. In some provinces, says Du Halde, you find them in every town, and even in the large villages. The most considerable of them all are the famous porcelain-tower at Nang-King †, and that of Tong-Tchang-Fou, both of which are very magnificent structures.

In regard to their form, the *Taas* are all nearly alike; being of an octagonal figure, and consisting of seven, eight, and sometimes ten stories, which grow gradually less both in height and breadth all the way from the bottom to the top. Each story is finished with a kind of cornish, that supports a roof, at the angles of which hang little brass bells; and round each story runs a

---

* The Chinese are very clever at these kinds of ornaments. In Plate VII. are designs of several of them: they are made in wooden moulds, of well tempered clay; and each figure, when large, is composed of several pieces, which they put together so neatly that the joints are scarce perceptible.

† Du Halde Vol. 1. p. 129. The porcelain-tower at Nang King is without doubt the highest and finest in China. It is of an octagonal figure, each side being fifteen foot. It is two hundred feet high, and divided into nine stories, by simple floors within, and by cornishes without, which sustain little roofs covered with green tiles.

Vol. 1. p. 200. Tong-Tchang-Fou is likewise celebrated for it's buildings; especially for a tower of eight stories, erected without the walls; the outside of which is of porcelain, adorned with divers figures, and the inside is lined with marble, of different colours, and finely polished. By a stair-case made in the wall you ascend to the different stories, and from thence to very fine galleries of marble, adorned with gilt iron rails, which embellish the projections wherewith the tower is surrounded. At the corners of these galleries hang little bells, which when moved by the wind make an agreeable tinkling.

narrow

narrow gallery, inclosed by a rail or balustrade. These buildings commonly terminate in a long pole, surrounded with several circles of iron, hanging by eight chains fixed to the top of the pole, and to the angles of the covering of the last story.

Fig. 1. Plate V. is copied from one of those towers, that stands on the banks of the Ta-Ho *, between Canton and Hoang-Pou. It is raised on three steps, and consists of seven stories. The first story is entered by four arched doors, and contains one room of an octagonal figure, in the middle of which is the stair that leads to the second story, as expressed in the plan fig. 2. Plate V. The stairs that lead to all the other stories are placed in the same manner; the cornishes that finish the different stories are all alike, and composed of a fillet and large cavetto, enriched with ornaments representing scales of fish; which is common in the Chinese buildings as well as in those of the ancients. The roofs are all turned up at the angles, and all but the lowermost are adorned with foliages and bells. The building is finished with a pole, at the top of which is a ball, and round it nine circles of iron suspended by chains fixed to the angles of the uppermost roof. I have omitted representing, in the elevation, the stairs that lead to the different stories, because it would have rendered the design confused.

OF
VARIOUS OTHER FORMS OF
BUILDING USED IN CHINA.

I HAVE already given an account of the three sorts of *Tings* which I saw in different temples at Canton. The fourth, which is used in their gardens, is represented in Plate VI. fig. 2. These buildings generally consist only of twelve columns, raised on a basement, and supporting a roof like those in Plate II. and fig. 2. Plate III.

THE building, from which I copied my design, stood in the middle of a small lake, in a garden at Canton; and I chose it for a model in preference to any other, on account of it's singularity.

IT is raised on a pretty high basement, surrounded with a rail, and composed of twelve columns, whose bases are very like a profile of Palladio's for the Thuscan base. These columns support the roof, on which is placed a lantern, finished with an ornament of which the hint is taken from the finishing on the *Taa*. The heads of all the columns are pierced by the beams of the

---

* Id est, Great River, which is the name given to the river that runs by Canton.

Of the Buildings of the Chinese. 7

roofs, the extremities of which are adorned with little mascarons and bells. In the intercolumnations under the great roof reigns a friez, ornamented with fretwork. For the proportions of the several parts see the design, and for the plan fig. 5. Plate V.

In the same Plate with the last mentioned design is another, copied from one I met with in a garden at Canton. It's plan fig. 3. Plate V. is the same as that of the Monopteros temple; but the elevation is different. It is composed of ten columns, that support a roof and lantern, covered in the form of a cone, and finished with a ball. The other particulars may be seen in the design, where they are accurately delineated.

In Plate VII. is the design of a bridge, the only one I saw in China, worth taking notice of; though from the accounts we have there are some in that country ‡ exceedingly magnificent. It stood in the garden of a merchant at Canton, and was all built of wood; excepting the parapet, which was of brickwork, and the piers, which were of stone covered with stucco, and scratched into irregular figures, as expressed in the design. This is a common manner of ornamenting among the Chinese.

The Päy-Leou, or triumphal arches, are very common in China: at Canton there are many of them; but I saw none that were fine. In Plate XI. is a design of one of them, which was the most tolerable I met with.

OF THE
HOUSES OF THE CHINESE.

THE houses of the Chinese are all distributed in one and the same manner. It would be impertinent, and even dangerous, to be singular in this respect. Le Comte mentions a Mandarin, who, having built a house more lofty and stately than the rest, was accused before the

---

‡ Du Halde Vol. 1. p. 31. The stone-bridges are most of them built, like ours, on large piers capable of breaking the force of the stream, having arches sufficiently wide and high for the largest barks to pass through. They are very numerous in China, and the Emperour spares no expence, when the benefit of the publick requires them to be built. There is scarce a more beautiful bridge to be seen than that of *Fou-Tcheou-Fou*, capital of the province of *Fo-Kien*. The river, which is half a league broad, is sometimes divided into small arms, and sometimes interspersed with little islands: All these are united by bridges which join the islands, and make together eight stades, or *lis*, and seventy six Chinese fathom. The principal bridge alone has above a hundred arches, built of white stone, and adorned with a balustrade, &c.

But that which surpasses all the rest is the bridge of *Suen-Tcheou-Fou*, built over an arm of the sea, which otherwise must be crossed in a bark, often not without danger. It is 2520 Chinese feet long and 20 broad, supported by 252 huge piers, 126 on each side, all the stones, as well those that cross from one pier to the other breadth ways, as those which bear on and join them, are of the same length, thickness and colour, which is greyish.

It is not easy to comprehend where they could find so many large pieces of rock, or how they could contrive to cut and place stones of such enormeous weight, on pillars high enough for large vessels to pass underneath. The bridge is likewise set off with ornaments made of the same sort of stone. In short, the most remarkable things to be seen elsewhere, however esteemed in the country, are nothing comparable to this.

Emperour,

Of the Buildings of the Chinese.

Emperour, and fearing the consequence, pulled it down while the affair was under consideration.

Plate VIII. fig. 1.

In the Chinese houses more than one half of the ground is taken up with courts and passages. At Canton the houses of the merchants are all built on the river side, narrow, and very long. The same disposition is observed in them all: on the ground floor a broad passage A, running from the street to the river occupies the middle; and on the sides are the apartments, each consisting of a large room B for the reception of visitants, a small bed-room C, and sometimes a closet or study D. Every apartment has before it a court E; at the farther end of which is generally a pond, or cistern of water, with an artificial rock placed therein, on which grow some bambou-trees*, and shrubs of different sorts; the whole forming a little landscape pretty enough: the cistern, or pond, is stocked with gold-fish, some of which are so tame, that they will come to the surface of the water, and feed out of one's hand. The sides of the courts are sometimes adorned with flower-pots, and sometimes with flowering shrubs, or vines, and bambous, that form arbours. In the middle is generally placed, on a pedestal, a large porcelain vase, in which grow those beautiful flowers called Lien-Hoa †; and in these little courts they frequently keep pheasants, Bantam fowls, and other curious birds.

Plate VIII. fig. 1. and Plate IX. which is a section on the line T thrown into perspective.

Plate VIII. fig. 1.

Plate X. fig. 2.

Plate X. fig. 1.

The large room or saloon B is commonly from eighteen to twenty four foot deep, and about twenty broad. The side towards the court just described is entirely open; having only a cane-mat, which lets down occasionally to keep out rain or sun-shine. It is paved with flags of stone or marble, of different colours: the side-walls are matted about three or four foot upwards from the pavement; the rest being neatly covered, either with white, crimson, or gilt paper: and instead of pictures they hang on them long pieces of satin or paper, stretched on frames, and painted in imitation of marble, or bambou, on which are written, in azure characters, moral sentences and proverbs, extracted from the works of their philosophers ‡. Sometimes too they have pieces of plain white paper, with large characters pencilled in Indian ink by some celebrated hand, which they esteem vastly. The bottom or further end of the room is entirely composed of folding doors, the upper part of which are of lattice-work, covered with painted gause, which admits light into the bed-room.

---

* A sort of hollow cane.

† These flowers grow naturally in lakes and marshy grounds: in the province of Kiang-Si, says Du Halde, they are very common. The Chinese esteem them much, and cultivate them with great care; by which means they become very beautiful. The flower, which is not unlike a tulip, shoots up above the surface of the water a yard or more: some of them are red and white, others violet, and some yellow and white: the leaves are very large, smooth, and shaped like a heart: they, as well as the flowers, are fastened to the root by very long stalks: some of them float on the surface of the water, and others rise above it. The smell of the flower is pleasant.

I brought several of these inscriptions with me from China, but neglected to get them explained. In Plate XVIII. are eight of them, which I sent to the Propaganda at Rome to be translated, and received the following interpretations in Italian of four of them; the rest could not be interpreted, two of them being Tartarian, and the copies I sent of the other two so incorrectly written that they were unintelligible.

fig. 1. Otto Mille Anni d'età, per far la Primavera.
- 2. Noventa Mille Anni, per far una legha intera.
- 3. Fumo di Thè produce una nube, che pur diletta.
- 4. Piccola Goccia, venticello sul pino fa tremar le frondi d'una Canetta.
- 5. } Tartarean.
- 6. }
- 7. } Chinese.
- 8. }

These

Of the Buildings of the Chinese.

These doors are neatly made of wood; have several characters and figures on them, and are sometimes richly varnished, in red, blue, yellow, and other colours.

Sometimes in the middle of this end of the room, over a table on which are placed several little ornaments, they hang a very large sheet of thick paper, covered with antique Chinese paintings, inclosed in pannels of different figures. These they hold in great veneration, imagining that those who painted them were inspired. The Chinese connoisseurs pretend to know the different hands, and pay considerable prices for such as are allowed to be originals. I have seen many of these paintings; they are commonly drawn with Indian ink on white paper, and represent either landscapes, or figures. They are generally touched with spirit, but too incorrect and slight to deserve much notice. Some landscapes, however, I have seen, the sites of which were admirably imagined, though they were very deficient in other respects.

The moveables † of the saloon consist of chairs, stools, and tables; made sometimes of rose-wood, ebony, or laquered work, and sometimes of bambou only, which is cheap, and nevertheless very neat. When the moveables are of wood, the seats of the stools are often of marble, or porcelain; which, tho' hard to sit on, are far from being unpleasant, in a climate where the summer heats are excessive. In the corners of the room are stands, four or five feet high, on which they set plates of citrons, and other fragrant fruits, or branches of coral in vases of porcelain, and glass-globes containing gold-fish, together with a certain weed somewhat resembling fennel. On such tables as are intended for ornament only, they also place little landscapes, composed of rocks, shrubs, and a kind of lilly that grows among pebbles covered with water: sometimes too they have artificial landscapes, made of ivory, chrystal, amber, pearls, and various stones. I have seen of these that cost a thousand tael §; but they are at best mere baubles, and miserable imitations of nature. Besides these landscapes, they adorn their tables with several vases of porcelain, and little vessels of copper, which are held in great esteem. These are generally of simple and pleasing forms*: the Chinese say they were made two thousand years ago, by some of their celebrated artists; and such as are real antiques (for there are many counterfeits) they buy at an extravagant price, giving sometimes no less than three hundred pounds sterling for one of them. They keep them in little paste-board boxes, never exposing them to view, but on particular occasions; and none but the owner is suffered to touch them, who from time to time brushes off the dust, with pencils made for that purpose.

Plate X. Fig. 1, 2.

But amongst the principal ornaments of these rooms are the lanterns; of which there are generally four suspended from the cieling by silken cords.

---

† In Plates XIII and XIV I have given designs of several tables, chairs, and stands; and in Fig. 1 and 2, Plate X, are various designs of stools.

§ Above 300 guineas.
* See the two figures at the bottom of Plate XVI, and the middle one at the top of Plate XV.

They

Of the Buildings of the Chinese.

They are made of a very thin silk, neatly painted with flowers, birds, and landscapes; being square, octagonal, aud of a great variety of other forms, some of them very pretty.

Plate VIII. Fig. 1.

THE bed-room C is divided from the saloon only by a partition of folding doors, as I observed before, which, when the weather is hot, are in the night thrown open to admit the air. It is very small, and contains no other furniture than the bed, and some varnished chests, in which they keep their apparel. The beds are sometimes very magnificent; the bedsteads made much like ours in Europe, of rose-wood carved, or laquered work; the curtains are of taffeta, or of gause; sometimes flowered with gold, and commonly either blue or purple. About the top a slip of white satin, a foot in breadth, runs all round; on which are painted, in pannels of different figures, flower-pieces, landscapes, and conversation-pieces, interspersed with moral sentences and fables, written in Indian ink and vermillion.

A PASSAGE on the side of the bed-room leads to the study D, which is always closed on every side with walls, and lighted with windows. The walls are hung with moral sentences, as in the saloon, and antique paintings; the moveables consist of elbow-chairs, couches, and tables: there are several shelves filled with books, and on a table, near the window, are placed in great order pencils, and other implements for writing, the instruments which the Chinese use in arithmetical computations, and some choice books.

BESIDES these apartments, the ground-floor contains the dining-hall F, the kitchen G, the couli's or servant's room H, the bath I, and the necessary-house K; the offices or compting-houses L, and towards the street the shops M.

IN this manner are distributed all the merchant's houses at Canton; and the houses of other persons differ only as they are forced to vary the general plan by the figure of the ground which they have to build on: but all have their apartments, courts, and other conveniencies, in the manner already described.

Plate VIII. fig. 2.

THE Leou, or upper story, consists of several large halls O, that occupy the whole breadth of the house, and cover the apartments on the ground-floor. These are occasionally converted into lodging-rooms for strangers P. In every house they have a provision of wooden leaves, or sliders, two or three feet broad, and ten or twelve long, which, when rooms are wanted, they fasten to the floor and cieling, and in a few hours form any number of apartments. Some of these sliders are open from the top to within four feet of the flooring, and, instead of glass, the open part is filled with very thin oyster-shells, sufficiently transparent to admit the light. All the windows in Chinese buildings are made thereof.

IN one of these large halls, usually in that nearest to the gate of the house, is the portrait and altar Q of the houshold idol, so placed as to be

seen

Of the Machines and Dresses of the Chinese.

I THOUGHT it needless to augment the number of the plates, by giving sections of each design, as they would exhibit nothing worth notice. The insides of the temples in Plates II and III are intirely plain; having no other ornaments than the idols: and the buildings in Plates IV, VI, and VII, have no cielings; the timbers that support the roofs being exposed, and framed on the same principles with those in Plate XII. The tower, Plate V, is likewise quite plain within.

OF SEVERAL
CHINESE MACHINES AND DRESSES.

PLATE XVII represents some Chinese boats, which I inserted in this work at the desire of several persons. They are indeed copied from a Chinese painting; but as the representations are exact, and the plate a supernumerary one, twenty only having been promised in the proposals, I presume no complaints will be made on that head.

In Plate XVIII are designs of some of their machines. Fig. 1 is a perpetual bellows, of an ingenious and very simple contrivance. It is composed of a box A, two foot long, about one broad, and one high: in it is a moveable board B, which is exactly fitted to the box, and, by means of the handle C, carried from one extremity to the other of the grooves D, D, in which it is fixed. At each end of the box is an opening E, E, against the inside of which hangs a leathern flap, or valve, for admitting fresh air; and in the front, near each extremity, is another opening F, F, fitted in the same manner, through which the air passes into the reservoir G, from whence it issues in a constant stream by the pipe H: for the board B being constantly moved backwards and forwards along the grooves D, D, the air is admitted without ceasing at one or other of the openings E, E, and forced in the same manner, by one or other of the openings F, F, into the reservoir G.

Fig. 2 represents an hydraulic machine, with which the Chinese peasants raise water to cover their rice-grounds. It's construction may easily be understood by the design: it is put in motion by a man's treading on the trusses A.

Fig. 3 is a machine for winnowing grain; the advantage of which is that it separates the best and heaviest from that which is of an inferior quality. The grain is put in at A, over which the bag is fixed in such a manner as to afford a constant supply: at B there is an opening, closed with a shutter D, which by means of the wedge C is raised or let down at pleasure: through this opening the grain falls; and the wheel E, being in motion, by the wind which it occasions drives the chaff out at F; the best grain, by reason of it's weight

weight, falling at G, while that of an inferior quality, being lighter, is carried to H.

In Plates XIX, XX, and XXI, are represented the different Dresses of the Chinese. Some of them were designed from the life; others were copied from the paintings of *Siou Sing Saang*, a celebrated Chinese master, whom, when I was at Canton, I employed to paint on glass all the Chinese dresses; and two or three of those in Plate XX were, to complete the collection, copied from some well executed models that I met with here in London: a liberty which, I hope, will be excused, as I know them to be exact representations.

Plate XIX. Fig. 1. A Co-Lao, or minister of state.
2. The Emperour in his robes.
3. An Eunuch of the imperial palace.
4. A Chinese Nun.
5. A Bonze in his robes of ceremony.
6. A country woman.

Plate XX. Fig. 1. A servant maid.
2. A military Mandarin.
3. A lady of quality.
4. A mendicant Bonze.
5. A peasant.
6. A lady of distinction.

Plate XXI. Fig. 1 and 2. Dress of the Chinese that live in boats on the water.
3. Winter-dress of the merchants, and other persons of note.
4. Summer-dress of the same.
5. A Mandarin of the law.

OF THE
ART OF LAYING OUT GARDENS
AMONG THE CHINESE.

THE gardens which I saw in China were very small; nevertheless from them, and what could be gathered from Lepqua, a celebrated Chinese painter, with whom I had several conversations on the subject of gardening, I think I have acquired sufficient knowledge of their notions on this head.

Nature

NATURE is their pattern, and their aim is to imitate her in all her beautiful irregularities. Their firſt conſideration is the form of the ground, whether it be flat, ſloping, hilly, or mountainous, extenſive, or of ſmall compaſs, of a dry or marſhy nature, abounding with rivers and ſprings, or liable to a ſcarcity of water; to all which circumſtances they attend with great care, chuſing ſuch diſpoſitions as humour the ground, can be executed with the leaſt expence, hide it's defects, and ſet it's advantages in the moſt conſpicuous light.

As the Chineſe are not fond of walking, we ſeldom meet with avenues or ſpacious walks, as in our European plantations: the whole ground is laid out in a variety of ſcenes, and you are led, by winding paſſages cut in the groves, to the different points of view, each of which is marked by a ſeat, a building, or ſome other object.

THE perfection of their gardens conſiſts in the number, beauty, and diverſity of theſe ſcenes. The Chineſe gardeners, like the European painters, collect from nature the moſt pleaſing objects, which they endeavour to combine in ſuch a manner, as not only to appear to the beſt advantage ſeparately, but likewiſe to unite in forming an elegant and ſtriking whole.

THEIR artiſts diſtinguiſh three different ſpecies of ſcenes, to which they give the appellations of pleaſing, horrid, and enchanted. Their enchanted ſcenes anſwer, in a great meaſure, to what we call romantic, and in theſe they make uſe of ſeveral artifices to excite ſurprize. Sometimes they make a rapid ſtream, or torrent, paſs under ground, the turbulent noiſe of which ſtrikes the ear of the new-comer, who is at a loſs to know from whence it proceeds: at other times they diſpoſe the rocks, buildings, and other objects that form the compoſition, in ſuch a manner as that the wind paſſing through the different interſtices and cavities, made in them for that purpoſe, cauſes ſtrange and uncommon ſounds. They introduce into theſe ſcenes all kinds of extraordinary trees, plants, and flowers, form artificial and complicated ecchoes, and let looſe different ſorts of monſtrous birds and animals.

IN their ſcenes of horror, they introduce impending rocks, dark caverns, and impetuous cataracts ruſhing down the mountains from all ſides; the trees are ill-formed, and ſeemingly torn to pieces by the violence of tempeſts; ſome are thrown down, and intercept the courſe of the torrents, appearing as if they had been brought down by the fury of the waters; others look as if ſhattered and blaſted by the force of lightning; the buildings are ſome in ruins, others half-conſumed by fire, and ſome miſerable huts diſperſed in the mountains ſerve, at once to indicate the exiſtence and wretchedneſs of the inhabitants. Theſe ſcenes are generally ſucceeded by pleaſing ones. The Chineſe artiſts, knowing how powerfully contraſt operates on the mind, conſtantly practiſe ſudden tranſitions, and a ſtriking oppoſition of forms, colours, and ſhades. Thus they conduct you from limited proſpects to extenſive views; from objects of horrour to scenes of delight; from lakes and rivers to plains, hills, and woods; to dark and gloomy colours they oppose such as are brilliant, and to complicated forms simple ones; distributing, by a judicious arrangement, the different masses of light and shade, in such a manner as to render the composition at once distinct in it's parts, and striking in the whole.

Where the ground is extensive, and a multiplicity of scenes are to be introduced, they generally adapt each to one single point of view: but where it is limited, and affords no room for variety, they endeavour to remedy this defect, by disposing the objects so, that being viewed from different points, they produce different representations; and sometimes, by an artful disposition, such as have no resemblance to each other.

In their large gardens they contrive different scenes for morning, noon, and evening; erecting, at the proper points of view, buildings adapted to the recreations of each particular time of the day: and in their small ones (where, as has been observed, one arrangement produces many representations) they dispose in the same manner, at the several points of view, buildings, which, from their use, point out the time of day for enjoying the scene in it's perfection.

As the climate of China is exceeding hot, they employ a great deal of water in their gardens. In the small ones, if the situation admits, they frequently lay almost the whole ground under water; leaving only some islands and rocks: and in their large ones they introduce extensive lakes, rivers, and canals. The banks of their lakes and rivers are variegated in imitation of nature; being sometimes bare and gravelly, sometimes covered with woods quite to the water's edge. In some places flat, and adorned with flowers and shrubs; in others steep, rocky, and forming caverns, into which part of the waters discharge themselves with noise and violence. Sometimes you see meadows covered with cattle, or rice-grounds that run out into the lakes, leaving between them passages for vessels; and sometimes groves, into which enter, in different parts, creeks and rivulets, sufficiently deep to admit boats; their banks being planted with trees, whose spreading branches, in some places, form arbours, under which the boats pass. These generally conduct to some very interesting object; such as a magnificent building, places on the top of a mountain cut into terrasses; a casine situated in the midst of a lake; a cascade; a grotto cut into a variety of apartments; an artificial rock; and many other such inventions.

Their rivers are seldom streight, but serpentine, and broken into many irregular points; sometimes they are narrow, noisy, and rapid, at other times deep, broad, and slow. Both in their rivers and lakes are seen reeds, with other aquatic plants and flowers; particularly the *Lyen Hoa*, of which they are very fond. They frequently erect mills, and other hydraulic machines, the motions of which enliven the scene: they have also a great number of vessels of different forms and sizes. In their lakes they intersperse islands; some of them barren, and surrounded with rocks and shoals; others enriched
with

with every thing that art and nature can furnish most perfect. They likewise form artificial rocks; and in compositions of this kind the Chinese surpass all other nations. The making them is a distinct profession; and there are at Canton, and probably in most other cities of China, numbers of artificers constantly employed in this business. The stone they are made of comes from the southern coasts of China. It is of a bluish cast, and worn into irregular forms by the action of the waves. The Chinese are exceeding nice in the choice of this stone; insomuch that I have seen several Tael given for a bit no bigger than a man's fist, when it happened to be of a beautiful form and lively colour. But these select pieces they use in landscapes for their apartments: in gardens they employ a coarser sort, which they join with a bluish cement, and form rocks of a considerable size. I have seen some of these exquisitely fine, and such as discovered an uncommon elegance of taste in the contriver. When they are large they make in them caves and grottos, with openings, through which you discover distant prospects. They cover them, in different places, with trees, shrubs, briars, and moss; placing on their tops little temples, or other buildings, to which you ascend by rugged and irregular steps cut in the rock.

When there is a sufficient supply of water, and proper ground, the Chinese never fail to form cascades in their gardens. They avoid all regularity in these works, observing nature according to her operations in that mountainous country. The waters burst out from among the caverns, and windings of the rocks. In some places a large and impetuous cataract appears; in others are seen many lesser falls. Sometimes the view of the cascade is intercepted by trees, whose leaves and branches only leave room to discover the waters, in some places, as they fall down the sides of the mountain. They frequently throw rough wooden bridges from one rock to another, over the steepest part of the cataract; and often intercept it's passage by trees and heaps of stones, that seem to have been brought down by the violence of the torrent.

In their plantations they vary the forms and colours of their trees; mixing such as have large and spreading branches, with those of pyramidal figures, and dark greens, with brighter, interspersing among them such as produce flowers; of which they have some that flourish a great part of the year. The Weeping-willow is one of their favourite trees, and always among those that border their lakes and rivers, being so planted as to have it's branches hanging over the water. They likewise introduce trunks of decayed trees, sometimes erect, and at other times lying on the ground, being very nice about their forms, and the colour of the bark and moss on them.

Various are the artifices they employ to surprize. Sometimes they lead you through dark caverns and gloomy passages, at the issue of which you are, on a sudden, struck with the view of a delicious landscape, enriched with
every

every thing that luxuriant nature affords most beautiful. At other times you are conducted through avenues and walks, that gradually diminish and grow rugged, till the passage is at length entirely intercepted, and rendered impracticable, by bushes, briars, and stones: when unexpectedly a rich and extensive prospect opens to view, so much the more pleasing as it was less looked for.

Another of their artifices is to hide some part of a composition by trees, or other intermediate objects. This naturally excites the curiosity of the spectator to take a nearer view; when he is surprised by some unexpected scene, or some representation totally opposite to the thing he looked for. The termination of their lakes they always hide, leaving room for the imagination to work; and the same rule they observe in other compositions, wherever it can be put in practice.

Though the Chinese are not well versed in opticks, yet experience has taught them that objects appear less in size, aud grow dim in colour, in proportion as they are more removed from the eye of the spectator. These discoveries have given rise to an artifice, which they sometimes put in practice. It is the forming prospects in perspective, by introducing buildings, vessels, and other objects, lessened according as they are more distant from the point of view; and that the deception may be still more striking, they give a greyish tinge to the distant parts of the composition, and plant in the remoter parts of these scenes trees of a fainter colour, and smaller growth, than those that appear in the front or fore-ground; by these means rendering what in reality is trifling and limited, great and considerable in appearance.

The Chinese generally avoid streight lines; yet they do not absolutely reject them. They sometimes make avenues, when they have any interesting object to expose to view. Roads they always make streight; unless the unevenness of the ground, or other impediments, afford at least a pretext for doing otherwise. Where the ground is entirely level, they look upon it as an absurdity to make a serpentine road: for they say that it must either be made by art, or worn by the constant passage of travellers; in either of which cases it is not natural to suppose men would chuse a crooked line when they might go by a streight one.

What we call clumps, the the Chinese gardeners are not unacquainted with; but they use them somewhat more sparingly than we do. They never fill a whole piece of ground with clumps: they consider a plantation as painters do a picture, and groupe their trees in the same manner as these do their figures, having their principal and subservient masses.

Of the Gardens of the Chinese.

THIS is the substance of what I learnt during my stay in China, partly from my own observation, but chiefly from the lessons of Lepqua: and from what has been said it may be inferred, that the art of laying out grounds, after the Chinese manner, is exceedingly difficult, and not to be attained by persons of narrow intellects. For though the precepts are simple and obvious, yet the putting them in execution requires genius, judgment, and experience; a strong imagination, and a thorough knowledge of the human mind. This method being fixed to no certain rule, but liable to as many variations, as there are different arrangements in the works of the creation.

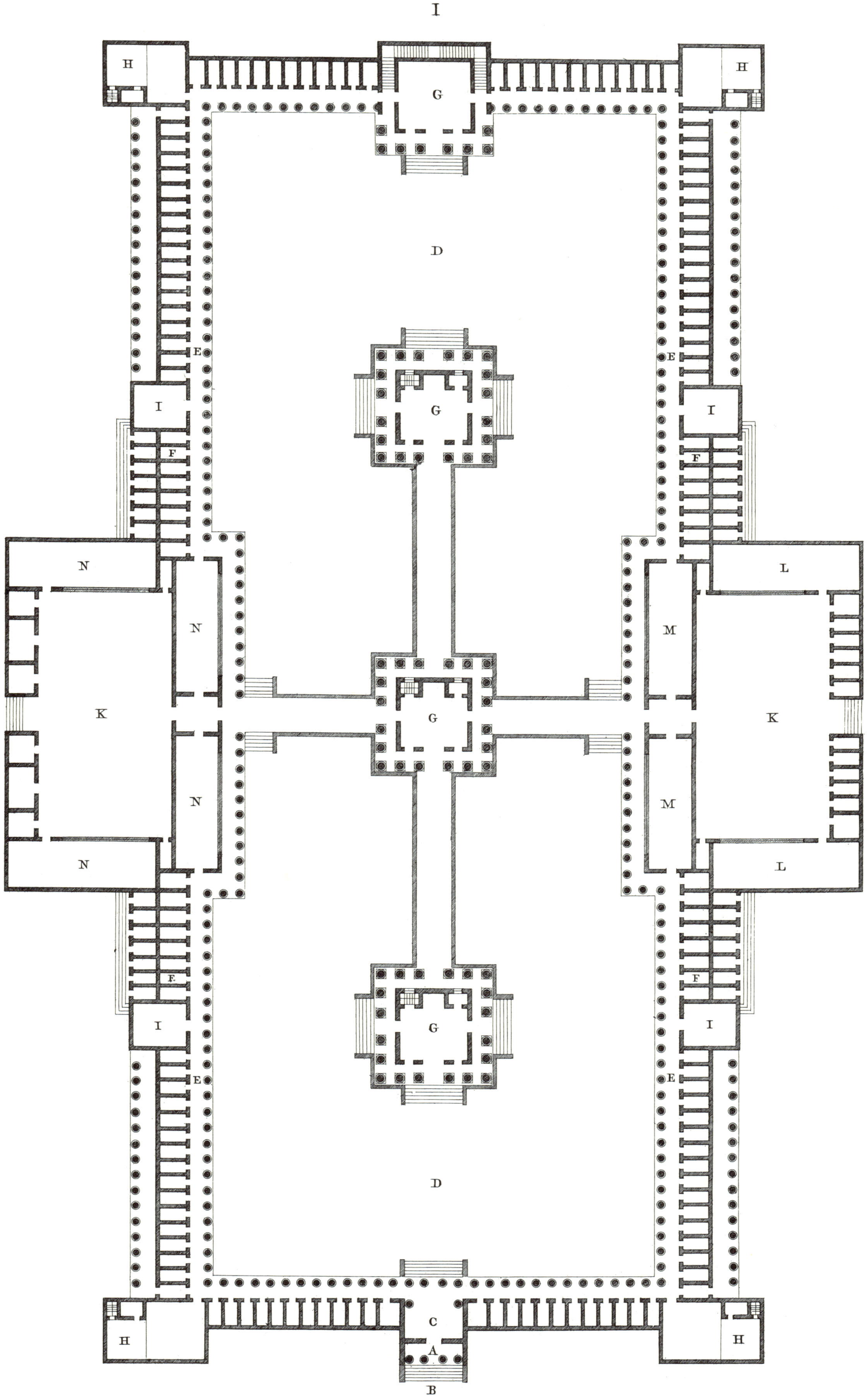

P. Fourdrinier Sculp.

II

III

1.

2.

P. Fourdrinier Sculp.

IV.

V.

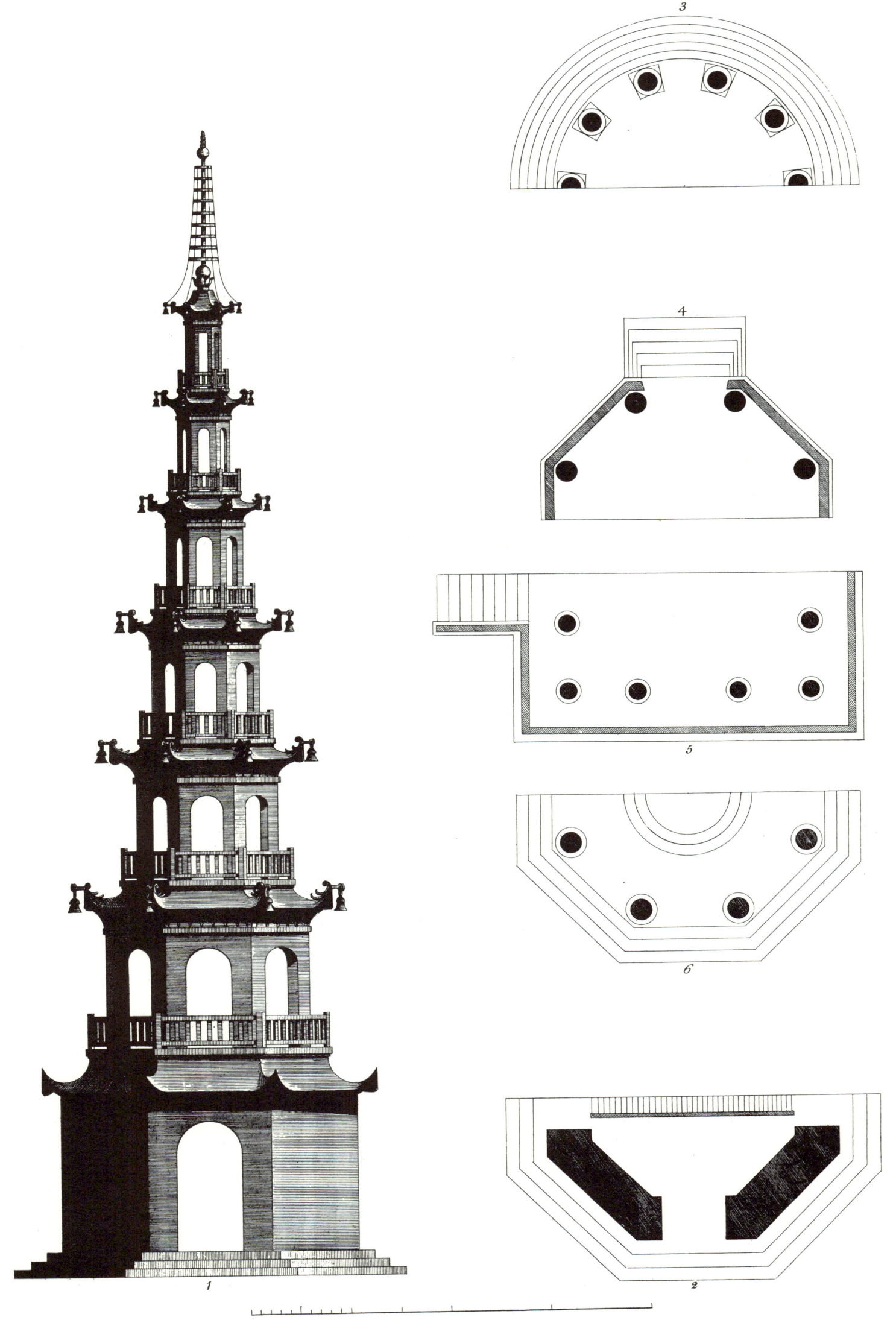

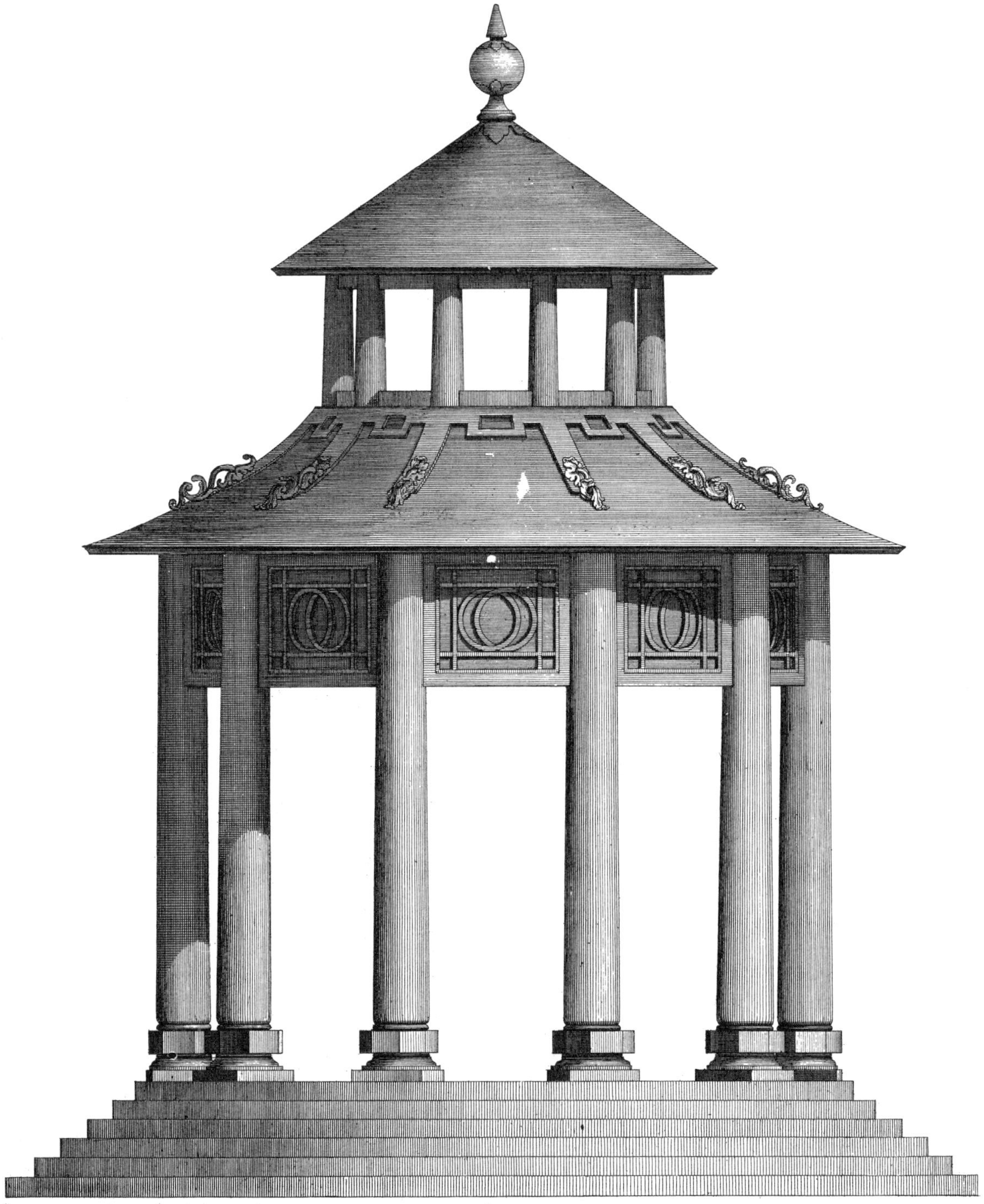

1

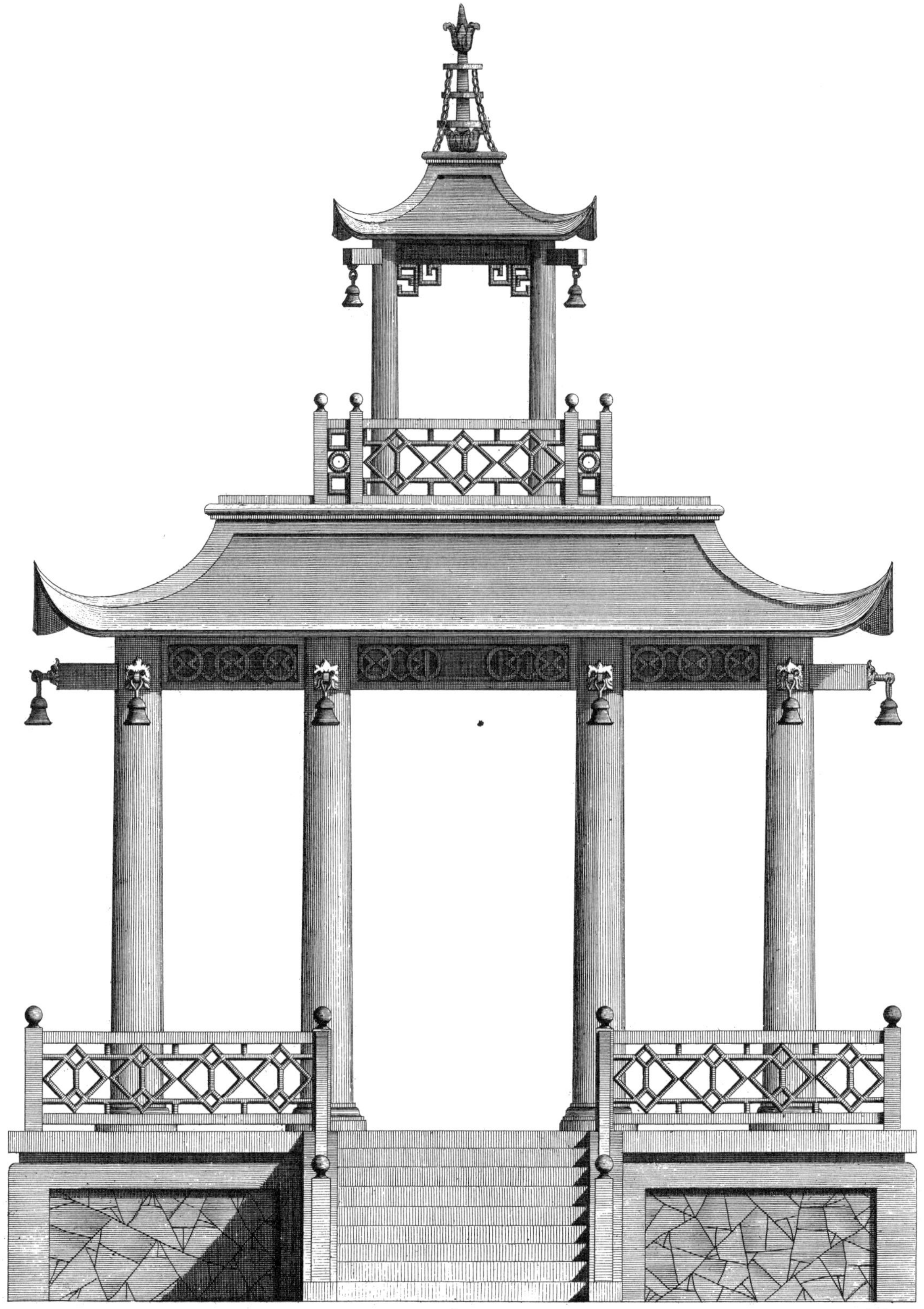

2

P. Fourdrinier Sculp.

VII

P. Fourdrinier Sculp.

VIII

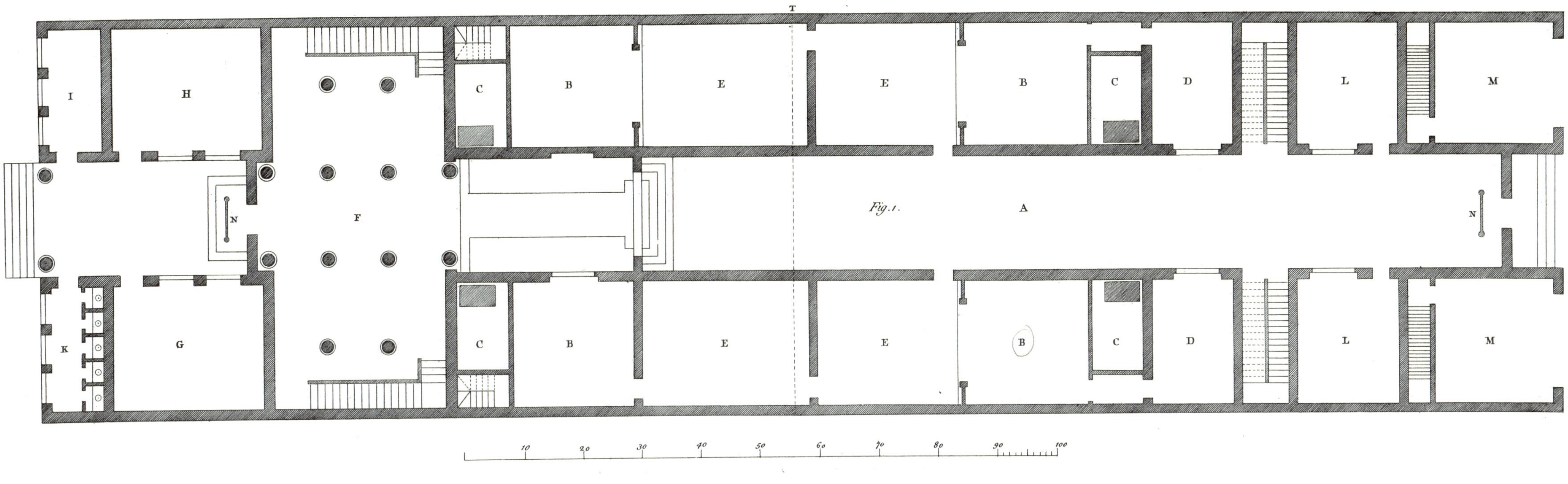

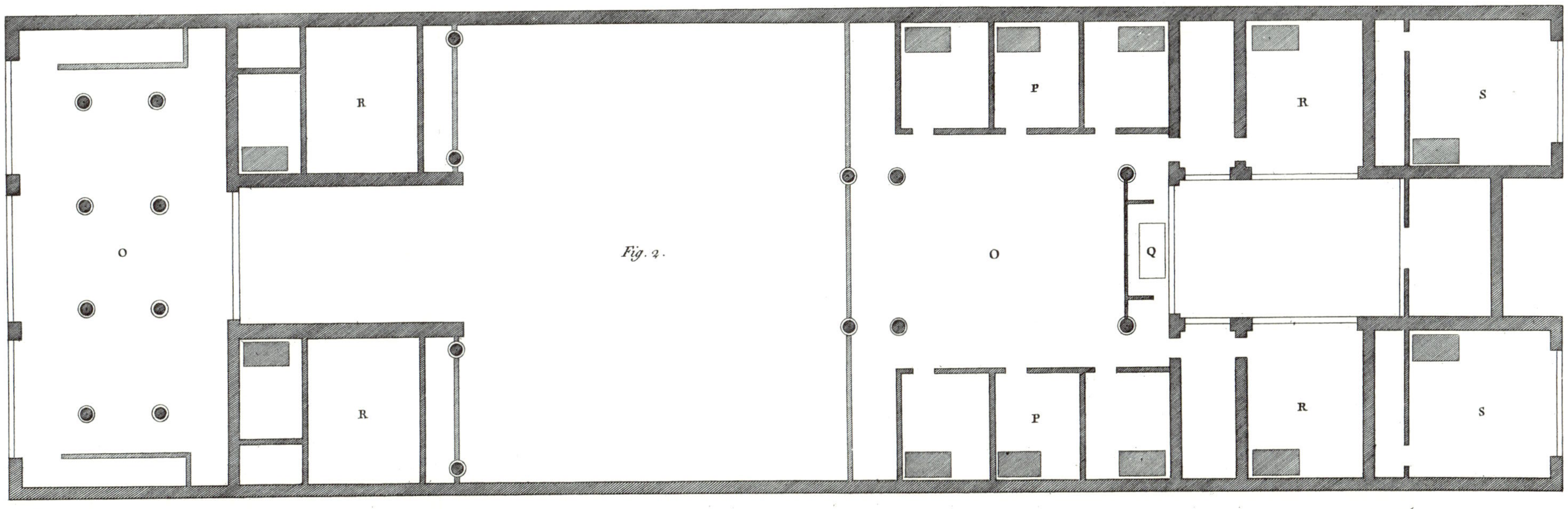

Fig. 1.

Fig. 2.

J. Fougeron Sculp.

XI

X

Fig. 1.

Fig. 2.

XI.

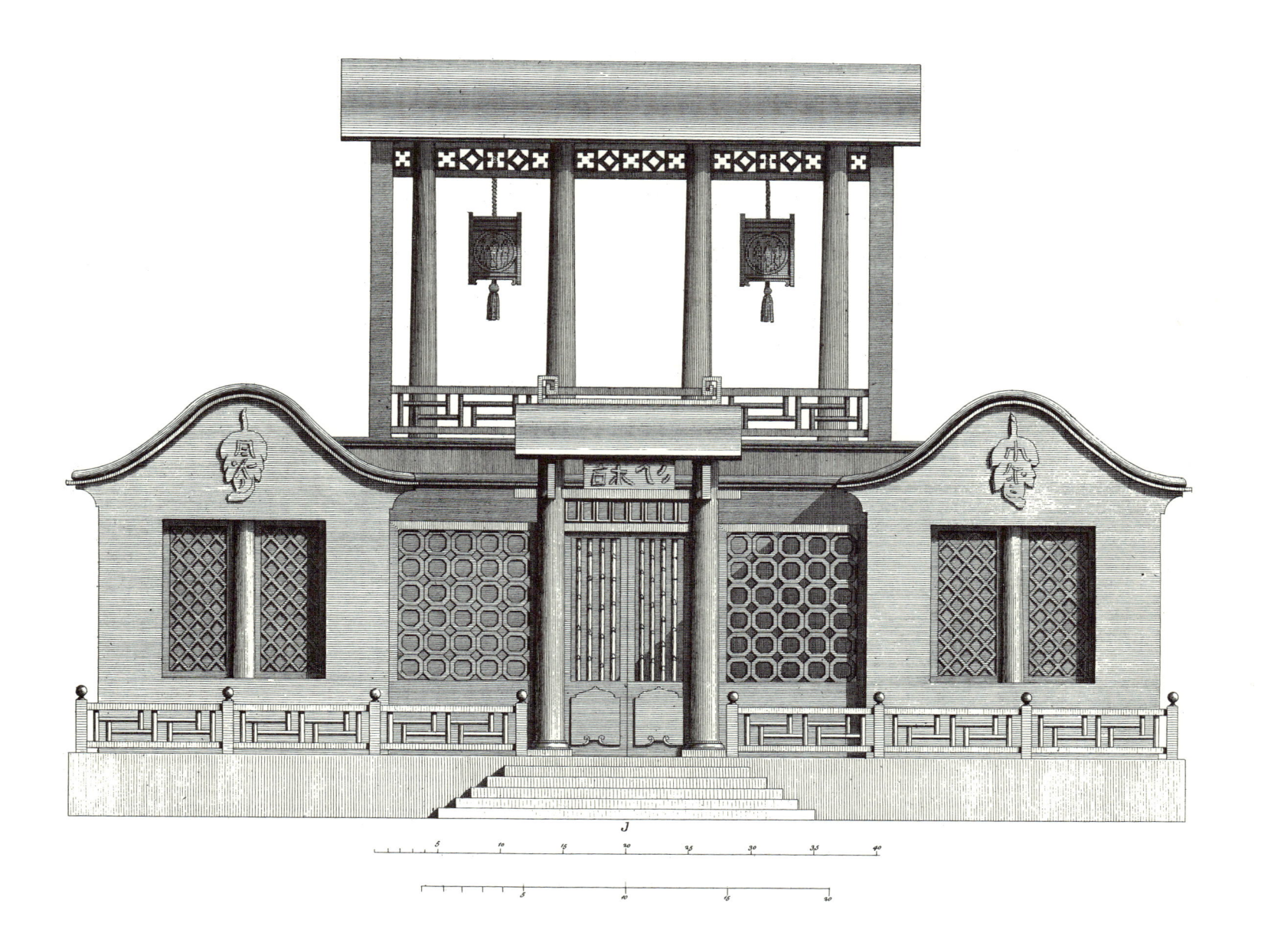

2

XII.

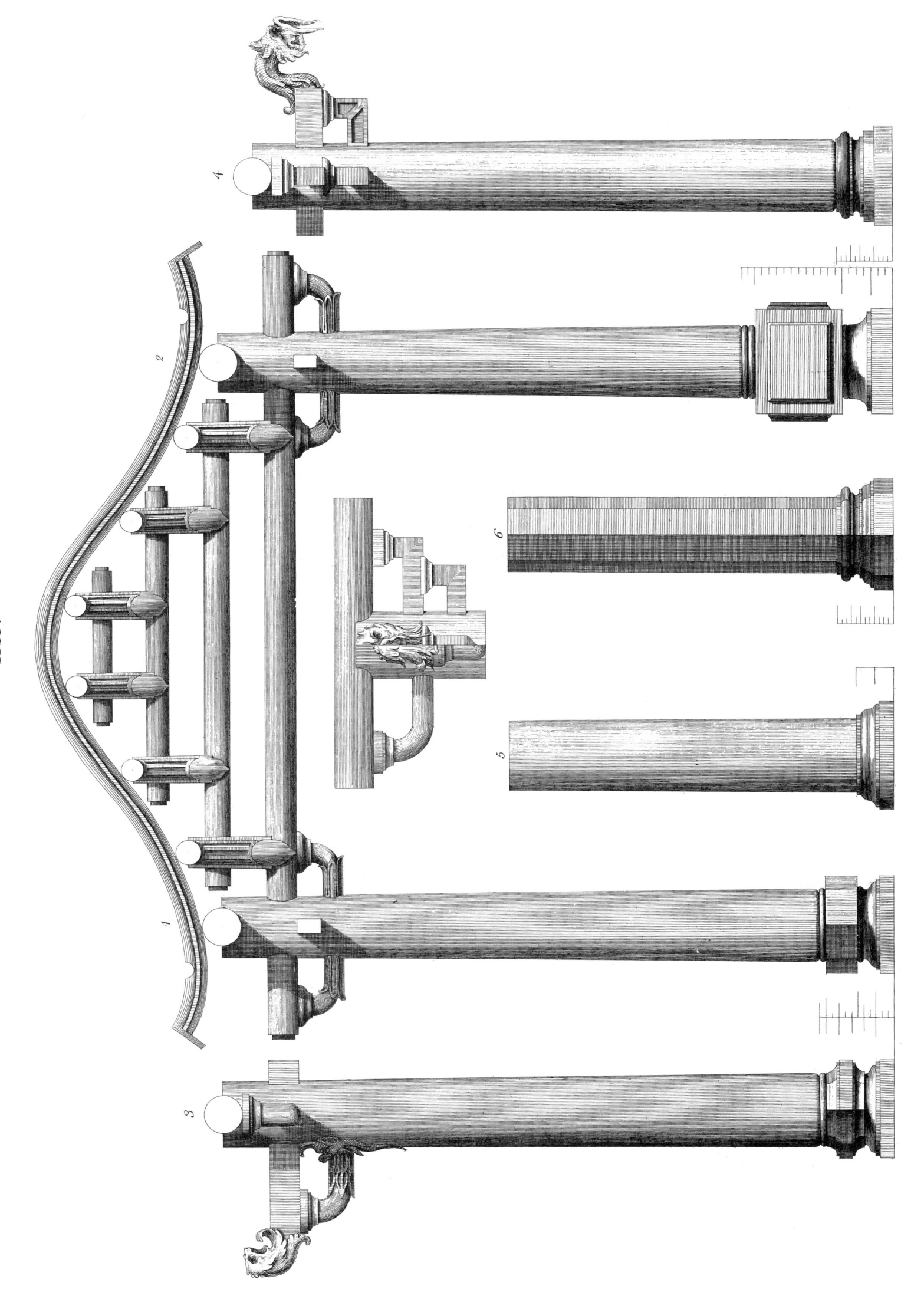

XIII

P. Fourdrinier sculp.

XIV

P. Fourdrinier sculp.

XV

P. Fourdrinier sculp.

XVI

XVII.

P. Sandby Sculp.

XVIII.

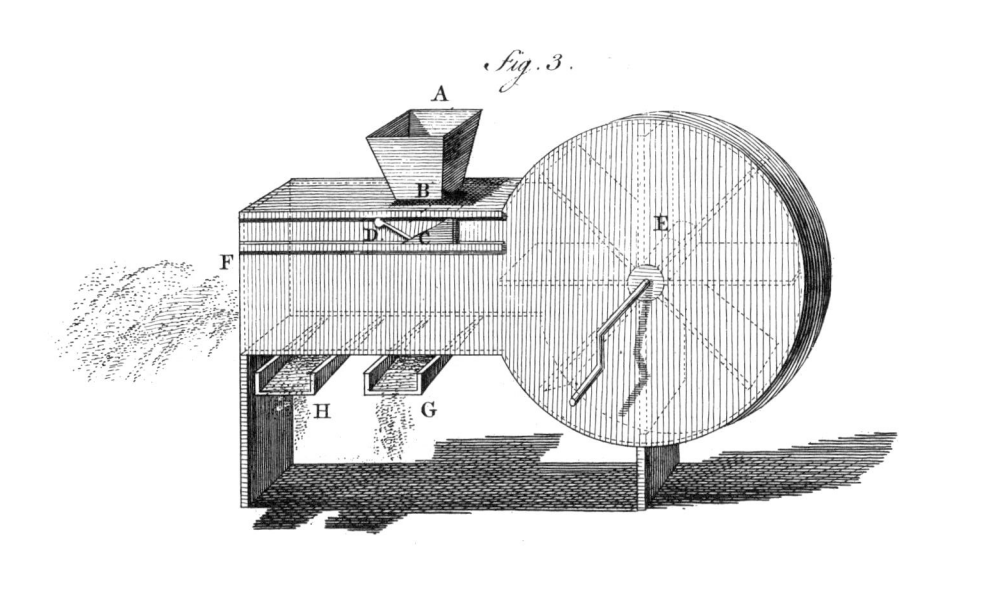

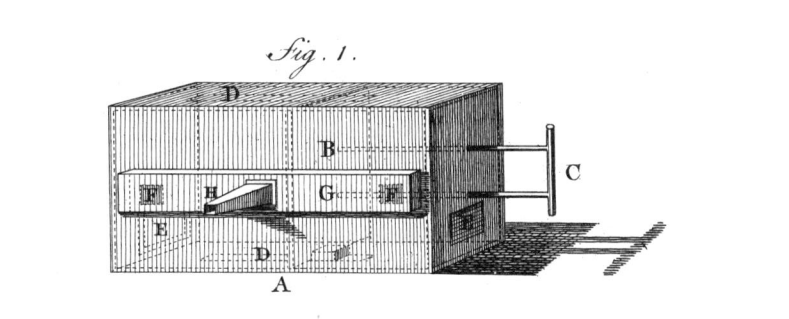

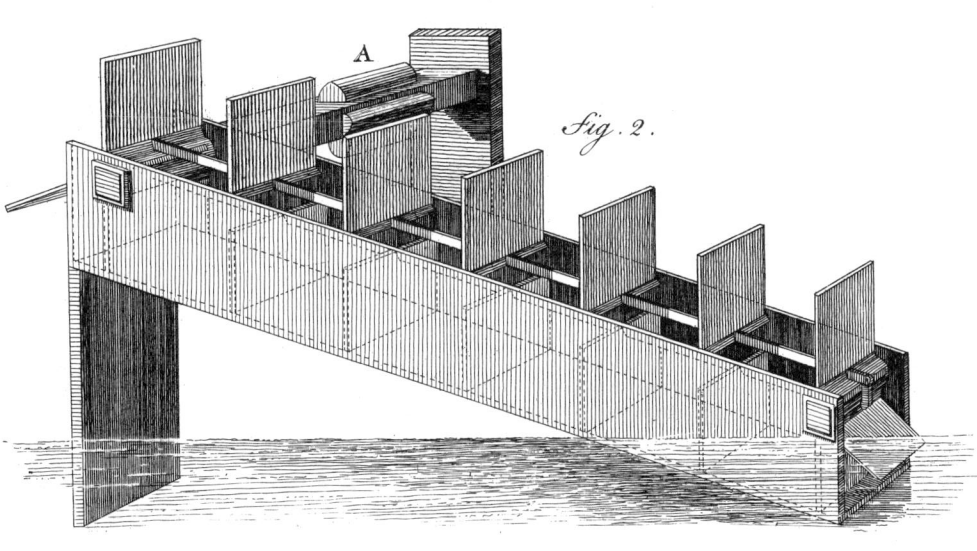

1. 春為歲首
2. 上而雨里濡北之
3. 降昏書貢琛烟茶
4. 米荈竹風松甫古
5. 覆与盒垛挼玉竹
6. 于鬯人色色地
7. 十送翠角荈雨
8. 八次鸟鳴埀

XIX

C. Grignion sculp

XX

1   2   3

4   5   6

C. Grignion sculp.

XXI

1

2

3 4 5

C. Grignion sculp.